The Rules of Bird Hunting

Eeva Park

About the translator

Jayde Will is a literary translator working from Lithuanian, Latvian, and Estonian. His recent or forthcoming translations include Daina Tabūna's short story collection *The Secret Box* (The Emma Press), Ričardas Gavelis's novel *Memoirs of a Life Cut Short* (Vagabond Voices), Artis Ostups's poetry collection *Gestures* (Ugly Duckling Presse), and Inga Pizāne's poetry collection *Having Never Met* (A Midsummer Night's Press). He lives in Riga.

The Rules of Bird Hunting

Eeva Park

Translated from Estonian by Jayde Will

Supported by the
Cultural Endowment of Estonia

EESTI KULTUURKAPITAL

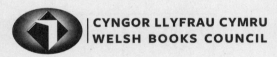

CYNGOR LLYFRAU CYMRU
WELSH BOOKS COUNCIL

Parthian, Cardigan SA43 1ED
www.parthianbooks.com
First published in 2018
© Eeva Park 2018
© Translation Jayde Will 2018
ISBN 9781912109081
Design and layout by Alison Evans
Printed by Pulsio

Contents

The Rules of Bird Hunting

On a bird hunt in early spring,
while learning the rules of hunting from old men,
don't forget to put your double barrel firmly on your shoulder.
The shot will knock you right on your back.
Then you'll be aiming straight at the sky,
and will hit your target this time as well
totally inadvertently
though it's not sight-corroding salt
that's making your eyes sting,
but a hail of shot,
cold white and painful.

If you've ever played
with a lizard on a big stone warmed by the sun,
caught him
every time he tried escaping,
and held him, captive, tail-less
under a sprat tin and awaiting the morning anew,
then you don't know anything yet about
the ants marching in a row
and afterwards it's already too late.

Tomorrow's News (or The Rise of the Rabbits)

Now, even the bunnies have turned evil.
They're roaring, biting hands,
ripping up the hay under their stomachs with their claws,
stomping their legs in the water bowl
and shitting chocolate-like chunks

The night of the long ears is coming.

The rabbits have risen up on their back legs.
A fear of judgment in their incandescent eyes
they look straight ahead,
listening,
to how the night snow transforms the morning raindrops
  into a battle drum.

Foxes in the vineyard
switch on their bubbling coffee machines
and read over and over again
all of yesterday's news.
Not a single line about the rabbits.

Singing

On an avenue of vanished trees
they make another nest
and sing on that misty morning.

Listen to them, listen.

Formica Rufa

The ant,
which I drained out of a birch juice jar
didn't die
nor was it dead,
though I killed it for the fifth time,
I squashed him to bits between the thumb and forefinger
of my right hand,
drowned him with tap water,
pressed him with a spoon,
but he climbed out of the sink,
dark brown and straight antennas
moving quickly on six legs
still in that one direction
a quick thought,
to grant him amnesty
I could toss him in the yard,
let him live,
if I could recognise his gait out of all
the other ants
I could be god of the ants.
But I don't.

An Invitation, For You

If you don't come now to my garden the almond tree and
    bullace will wither
the bird cherry scent will vanish
if you don't come
the plum blossoms will fall off and in the spring light of the
    old apple trees
dandelions' dead bodies will fly in the cool morning breeze
if you don't come quickly
the huge peony blossoms will open
the jasmine and grass and first strawberries will give off their
    scent
if you don't come
I will gather currants from the bushes for fermented wine
to bubble up the bloodstream's pulse
and I will take the potatoes out of the fields full of mouse
    nests
if you don't come quick
you will think that I am just a poor liar
in an empty bare garden
in the middle of mud and hoarfrost nights
if you don't come
the clear summer wine will run out
which gives the pollen closed in the peonies' heart a snowy
    taste

when you do come

House Pet

Today I am the king's cat
I walk in the hundred rooms of his castle
I sleep on the cushion of his throne
wearing a little watch of gold around my neck
I give off sparks, when his hand glides over my fur
I purr in the warmth of the canopy bed my claws
caress his body
only there where it itches
only there
I extend them
roaring in the jungle of my heart
where tigers tearing the habitat's trees
apart with their claws marking their territory
the dangerous limits of life

A Summer Dream

A cloud shepherd
watches over little lambs
in a glowing blue
leads the mellow wanderers
to drink
from the fiery source of the sun

Shadows on the earth
glide in the growing wheat

Above
in the light
the shepherd's spring

I read the rain.
All of its stories
are round.
Drip, drop, drip…

In the light of milky mornings
in the cold fog of the receding snow
dogs keep watch over the sun
in a young apple orchard

On Easter Sunday

The seeds
have sprouted,
the radishes have risen!

For Starters

God didn't banish
anyone.
He was the one who left
leaving us on our own in Eden,
leaving us everything—
all of this wretched paradise.

Fragile Islands

We carve up the darkness
from the beginning we build
islands of light
out of bonfires
oil lamps
candle flames
glowing light bulbs gleaming colourful ads ribbons
in the neon glow of the streetlights
the lighting of a match
in your cupped palm
we build islands of light
that are not left behind

Maybe the thing really is now simply in
refined movements
familiar tenderness
a body in free play
without that wild shame
that I once felt
because you were so beautiful

we went on our way singing, though you
couldn't sing the melody
and I
didn't know the words

we didn't try to reach our destination,
it didn't even come to mind

we simply went
to a place we could stop in each other
and each shrub fit
and haycock at the sides of the road

we went around and at random
and still without getting lost
because on the way you learned the melody
and I the words

but as evening comes the dust
of the road scratches our throats
I think the sadness of the quiet
that has touched down comes from that

I think

I think,
I know,
I am almost completely sure:
he loves me thanks to the mosquitoes,
because when we lie down naked
in the first cool morning breeze
they come and bite
me only,
never him,
him never ever,
so itching my entire body
I scratch myself till it starts to bleed
and when I wake up my left cheek is swollen
from their poison,
he only smiles,
because he
doesn't have one blemish
from the night's blood wedding
or the mosquitoes buzzing in the dark,
who come and bite
me only
never him,
him never
ever.

I am who I am
shameless deceitful timid
and still you water me
with your morning light

We ride on a carousel without music
you and me
we gallop around on our wooden horses
and everything that you tell me
goes to the wind
and everything that I shout to you
remains unanswered
we gallop on our wooden horses
and around us
is a land breathing silently
buds aching to be leaves
seeds straightening into trees
trees touching the wandering clouds

From Here to There

When you've packed your things for your trip
emptied your drawers and secret hiding spots
found your best clothes
and put it all in your borrowed suitcase
you realise that you can't take everything along,
that the suitcase weighs almost too much—
you can't even budge it from its spot
and you have to start all over
dump everything you have on the floor
and decide it's all too much
what you don't need at all
and what's missing
as you step out on your road

Spectrum

Say something nice.
Even a fib.
So what if I don't believe you,
that people shine,
say something about this light, that surrounds them
like a flame's glow from a candle
and when you saw the glimmer of all the seven colours
with glasses
and without
and believing
and not believing your own
eyes and power of sight
and the fact that others don't see it,
that they don't shout from surprise,
don't jump from their seat
looking, how the person in front of them is shining
in this triumphant light,
which surrounds him like a glow of a flame from a candle.

You lose everything—
gloves from your pocket
and the book you stopped reading last night,
though they're laying where
you put them yourself
and right in the middle of feverish searching,
which always begins
with looking from the wrong end,
you semi-accidentally realise my presence as well
and it's like that every day
you demand again and again,
that I give back everything
that belongs to you—
your lost gloves, your books, your winter boots and your dreams.

A good position for dreaming is what you're looking for
and you look for it over and over again
on your stomach, back, side,
your leg on my leg,
breathing in and out,
holding each other tight,
and then so far apart
as if we hadn't even met ourselves yet.

You row,
teeth clenched,
but I'm not a boat,
I'm a sail.

Unfurl me and go!

I walked with you to the ends of the earth,
to the shores of a garbage sea
and can't come back anymore.
The stench pursues us
and that ranting beggar,
who didn't believe,
that we didn't have anything more to give him.

One body in solitude cries out and another answers.
Our bodies never once doubted.
The skin realised and understood, when you came and we
    stayed,
Our skin pattern's exact match,
just like grass to a landscape, trees and hills and
an ever – changing sky above them.
the skin realised,
the bodies never once regretted,
if thoughts hadn't wallowed in pains of longing to get away,
then nothing would have chopped us apart.

Clarity

When you look at the sea
there are ships in your eyes

I only see water and foam
a cut-off line
on the border of the sky and sea

In the deepness of your eyes
two ships recede into the distance

Along with the snow came silence
and in that silence
                        something else
it slowly covered us
                        layer by layer
while we were on the path
the start of it had been left long ago
and the end was not yet ahead
We went
            a line of footprints
were left on the snow
                        along with something else

Somewhere

Somebody somewhere is always having
a good time
somebody somewhere
is always happy
talks smiles dances
sings with eyes glimmering
as you stand alone at the window with a toothbrush in hand
and listen to the buzz of the grey night mosquitoes somewhere
somebody
is always

having

a good time

Inheritance

There are twenty-two keys
on this keychain,
there are big ones, small ones, there are so many,
as my grandmother didn't manage to show
all the doors, chests and drawers
to my mother and I know even less than her,
I fumble around for it, try to understand
with my fingertips almost like a thief
what might fit where,
I try to see if it turns,
if the bolt locks again,
if it clicks,
if it opens,
or if it stays closed before me till the end of time.

Just like you
I had a mother
and a father as well.
Otherwise I wouldn't be here.
But why was I necessary
I don't know,
because they existed without me after all
and that's why I asked them,
why me, tell me
if you still remember,
why

Guardian Angel

While making a passport photo
You're told to raise your left shoulder
while looking at the camera lens.
You're leaning to one side
It's always been like that,
Though you don't feel it yourself, you don't know,
The photographer notices right away how
the weight falls on your left shoulder,
he adjusts you,
because it isn't balance,
that he came here to bring you,
definitely not.

The Object

A study of melancholy was conducted.
A team drawn up.
A project manager appointed,
root causes of depression investigated,
measured the general signs of continued stress,
sorrow and blood pressure weighed,
cholesterol
eyesight
shaking of hands
kidneys,
heart examination by ultrasound
and I saw
lying naked with gel on the left breast
how
the first being from the depths
of the earth's first sea pulsated on the blue screen
in a flaming volcano eruption.

Sworn Statements

It's easy at the beginning
because a kid is a kid is a kid, but
then she starts to realise,
that she will become a woman trickling blood and milk,
though she doesn't believe it, she decides
she knows what she's doing,
pours sugar from her cupped hands for a row of ants,
checking out the bustle, measuring their loads,
needles twice their size,
and thinks, that there is all the time in the world,
that she probably doesn't want to get married because it's
not going well for the men at all because
they have to live together with those women,
but the ants and her
definitely not.

I'm a rope made of veins
dragged across the city
I'm the one walking on the rope,
I don't even know,
what brought me there,
I don't even know,
why I'm staggering there.
A cutting cold breaks me into crystals,
I fall into pieces
against a foggy dream.
Never ever will I sleep again,
wake me up right away
before that dream.

Fear is that moment,
when masks fall away
and behind them
an eyeless emptiness keeps watch,
a rusty chain of wishes
dangling between dirty nails—
a dangerous bridge from today to tomorrow.

St. John's Night

The point of the matter is that the scar would remain
for your whole life,
so if you let the glowing poker
burn the mark of St. John on your back
while chewing a shashlik spit to numbness
so the cries of pain wouldn't ring all over Värska
then the point of the matter
precisely is
that the scar would remain.

Pennies from the Sky

You take a ten-cent coin from the ground
and put it in your pocket,
it doesn't matter whether it's on the muddy supermarket
   carpet at the entrance,
because it still shines like buried silver,
the paws of the three lions on the coat-of-arms ready to
   strike on one side
proving by its own destiny that
the least likely thing
can become a possible
everyday
means of payment squashed into the mud,
which in the end
you can't get anything with
other than a penny of happiness jingling
in the bottom of your pocket.

A Moment

Why does a particular moment stick in our memory intact
in water rippling past time
it's nothing important, at the beginning,
though as time passes it grows inside of you
and transforms and ever more plainly
as that moment of long ago, it's not the past for a moment
rather the same scents, colours, ripple of feelings,
a moment that's transient,
unchangeable,
eternal.

Panic

And what will happen now?
When there's no electricity.
The screen is black
And there is no light to be seen in the whole village.
Everything is quiet,
even what I didn't notice before the murmuring.
That also goes for the radio in the kitchen.
And now?
What will happen to me?
In this quiet twilight.
That very word almost slipped my mind.
I sit listening.
I sit oddly.
Time stands still.
For the moment. For the century.
And that is happening now?

Really, I know how to do different things,
Grow cabbages, roses and carrots—
they are sub-par every year,
both in dry times and when it rains
I don't have the right land for them, they grow all hairy,
but I know how to do other things
knit a jumper, make cement with just the right mixture,
clean a fish net,
I know how to clean
wounds also—
cuts and burns
and make mashed potatoes so there aren't any lumps,
and make a creamy pudding for dessert, that too,
but I know how to do other things too,
mend trousers and stretch an old, soaked beret that's
the size of a fist back into shape so it's tight on your head
no really,
I know how to ski, but not how to ice skate, though I know
how to do other things too
though you don't believe me anymore
I know how to do totally different things—
things that aren't useful to anyone,
edible or gettable
I just know how to be,
though not at all as well as I could,
if it were necessary to know
but somehow I still know
simply how to be.

A Promise

When I die,
Let it be only from love.
That's what I decided,
That's how the bonfires smelled
in the autumn yards in Nõmme,
where they didn't make compost
from the falling leaves
but fire.
They hadn't banned it by law yet,
they didn't take them out in black bin bags
to landfills outside the city limits,
I was still sure,
that when I die,
then it would only be from burning love.

Death came from the woods
with rubber boots on
the crazed howling of the dogs
made me go to the yard
she stood and looked at
our home
the ugly and haggard master
waved her hand
and everything became quiet
the sound of my heart
the pounding stopped
though she didn't see me
it was probably dark
she shouted and shouted an unknown name
I almost replied
I almost knew
it should be me, yes me
but then in the beam of the headlights
I stood with my hands full of the darkness of night
you brought bread and the kids from school
calling me from the empty yard
into the house

✖✖✖

When I lose words from time to time
a white fear does a dance in front of my eyes—
what will happen then
when all that residue remains there
and starts to eat away
at me from inside

We approach evening
through leafless trees
over a darkening land
I plunge my fingers into the cooling air
There's time to start a fire
close the door
before the night
turns the window into a black mirror
that cracks
from the icy light of the stars and far-off wailing of a dog

In the Year of the Lord

I think about money all the time
That I don't have it.
I measure a phone call's length
Not its content
I try to be very brief
And I start to st-st-stutter
For the first time in my life
I can't spit out a word
I think about money
I turn it between my fingers
I hold the last coin under my tongue
So it could be put on my eyelids
Fearing that otherwise
I will be buried with my eyes wide-open
I think about
How expensive it will
all be
I think of the round
zero
behind all of life's debts
I am thinking all the time

During the last five years
time has been speeding up
with the addition of the flu, ringing in my ears, pneumonia,
radiculitis, a trumpet, drums, glaucoma, high blood pressure,
the timpani ring
in the end a whole orchestra
plays such a mindless tune

I hung the clothes on the drying rack,
Pushed my shoes off,
Stepped on the scale three times in a row,
And it became clear,
That my heart is heavier and heavier and heavier and...

Now I should make jam
The plums are ready
Autumn is ready
I'm not

✖✖✖

Now since
the well is empty
I've started to love the
rain

✕✷✕

They are all so different
in this picture,
they now are
all equally deceased
they were so different in their good and bad ways
one of them was even a particularly vain scoundrel
he's also now like all the rest
they're all the same
they are

✖✖✖

Then it happens
your fingertips are strangely so sensitive
right from the morning
the coffee with milk tastes like poison
there isn't a seat in the bus
Two big children with dead eyes stumble right
in front of you on Harju street
in order to share their rack of illusions with you
they break your wrist almost by accident
take lunch money, your cell phone, electricity, water and
   longing for spring
shouting a greeting used since time immemorial by the dead
morituri te salutant

The party is ending
but there's one person
I'd like to see again
though the waiters in their black jackets gather up the
    leftovers
pack up the dishes and glasses,
though in place of the turned-down music every one of us is
    humming our own tune
and the sheep fade one by one

In the sad crew of the last party-goers
none of us is smiling anymore

On the Long Bench

The old beautiful women said come over
and sit here with us on the long bench
we'll make room for you in the middle
because when we go
through the dark from here
you'll have to stay
put your hands on your knees
and say
I am a beautiful old woman
on a long bench
at the edge of this world

Parthian Baltic Poetry

PARTHIAN

www.parthianbooks.com